HALLOWEEN Scribbles Drawing and Coloring Book

Are you ready to unleash your inner creative genius?

In this book you will find a collection of 20 randomly drawn scribbles waiting for you to turn into ghoulish works of art.

A great way to relax and wind down after a long day. Grab your coloring pencils, felt pens and a glass of wine and get into the de-stress zone.

I have put all the drawings on one side of each page so you can freely use felt pens without ruining a drawing on the other side. But if you do intend to use felt pens I highly recommend placing a sheet of paper under the page you are coloring to prevent accidental bleed through onto the next drawing.

The challenge is on!

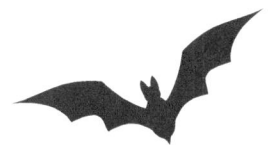

Copyright © 2018 www.paulscottondesign.com
All rights reserved.
ISBN-13: 978-1726297714
ISBN-10: 1726297713

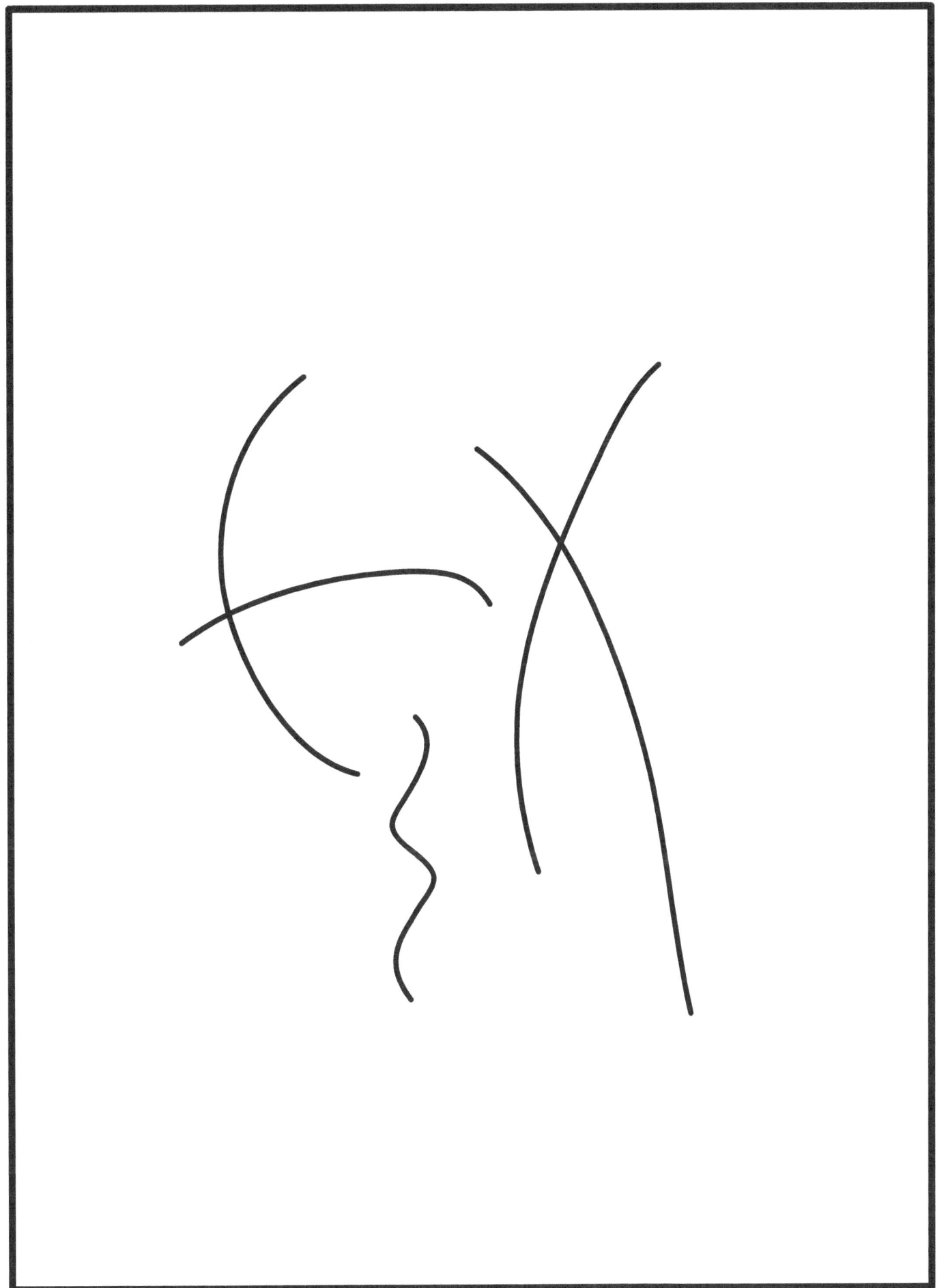

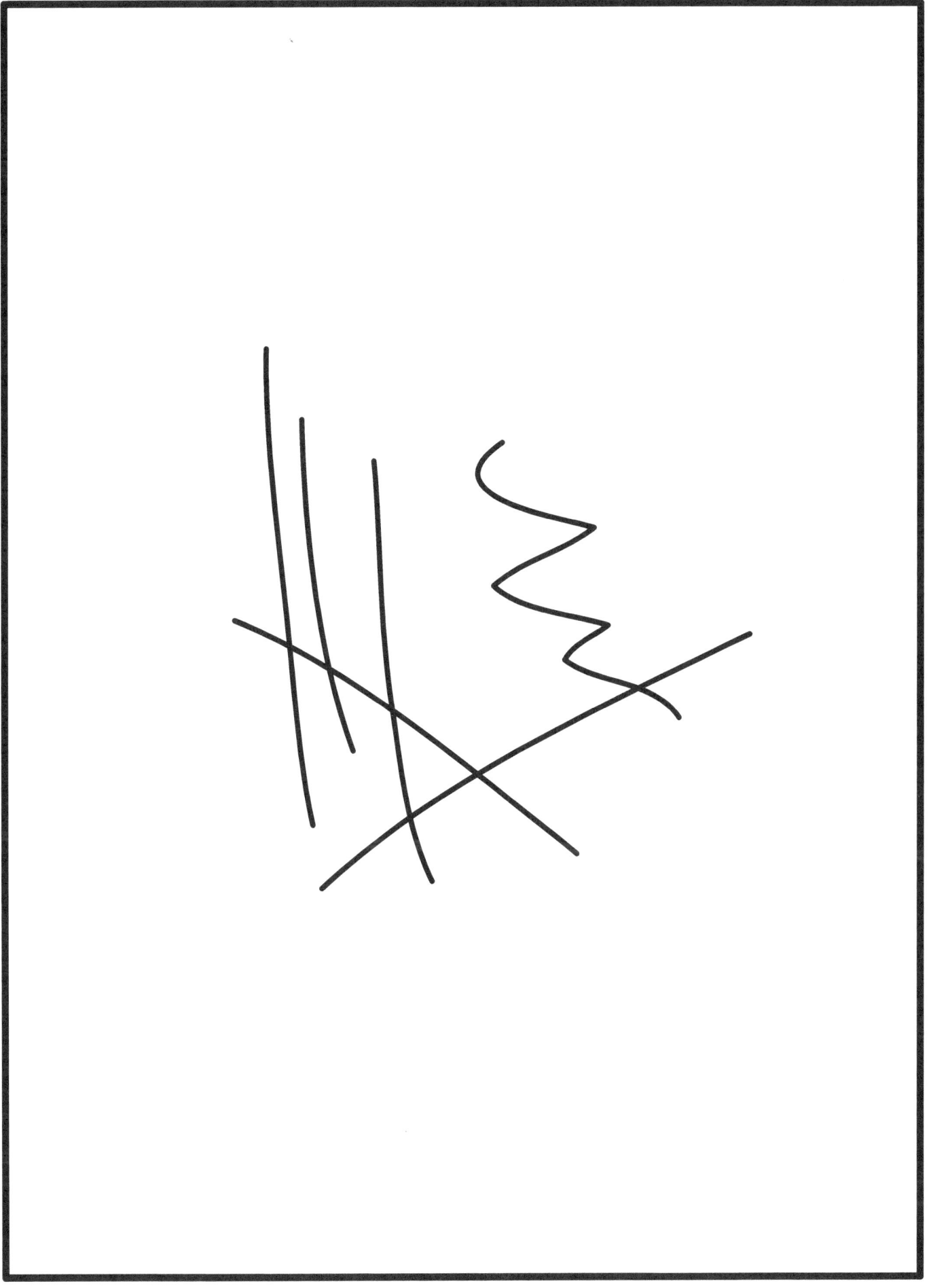

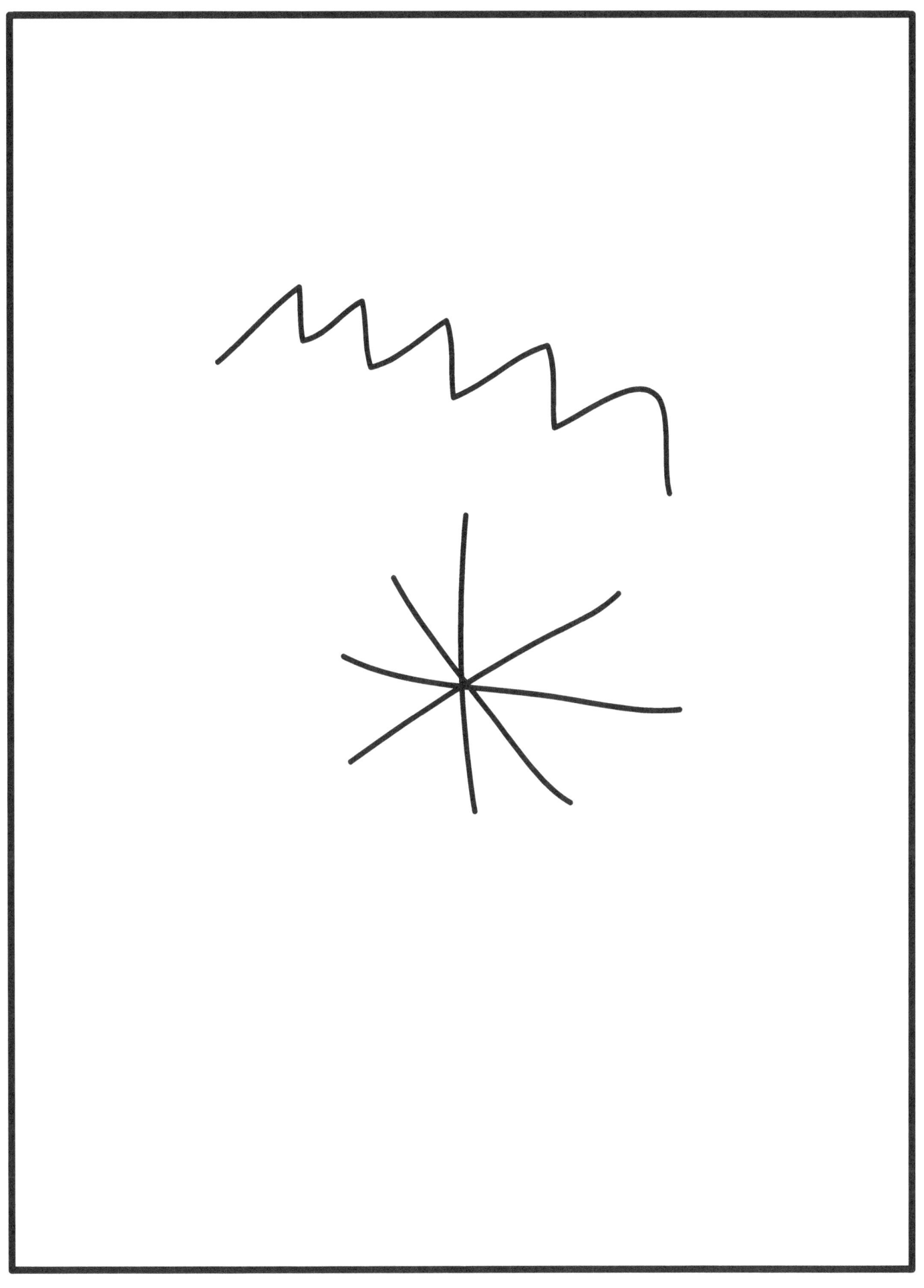

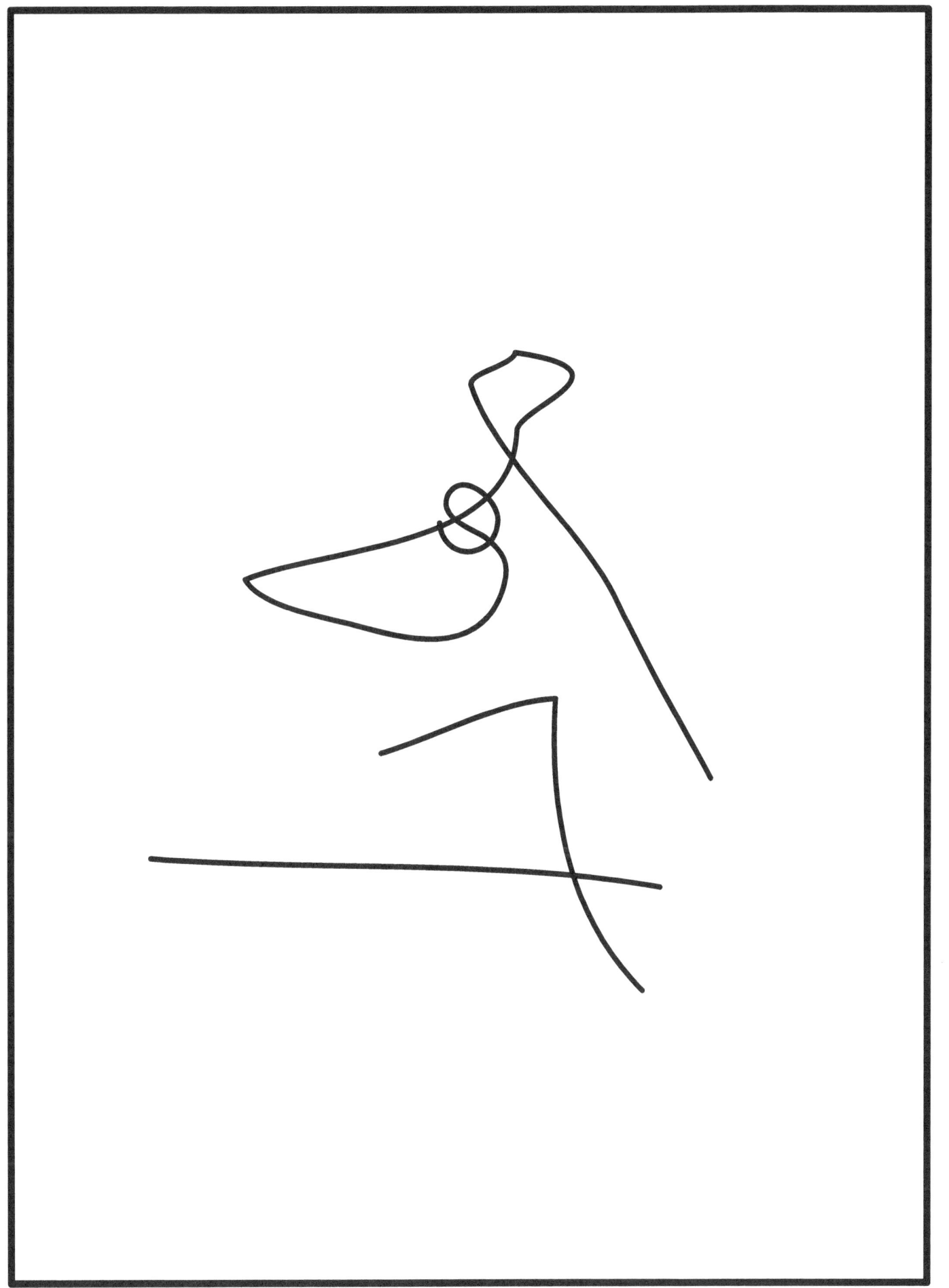

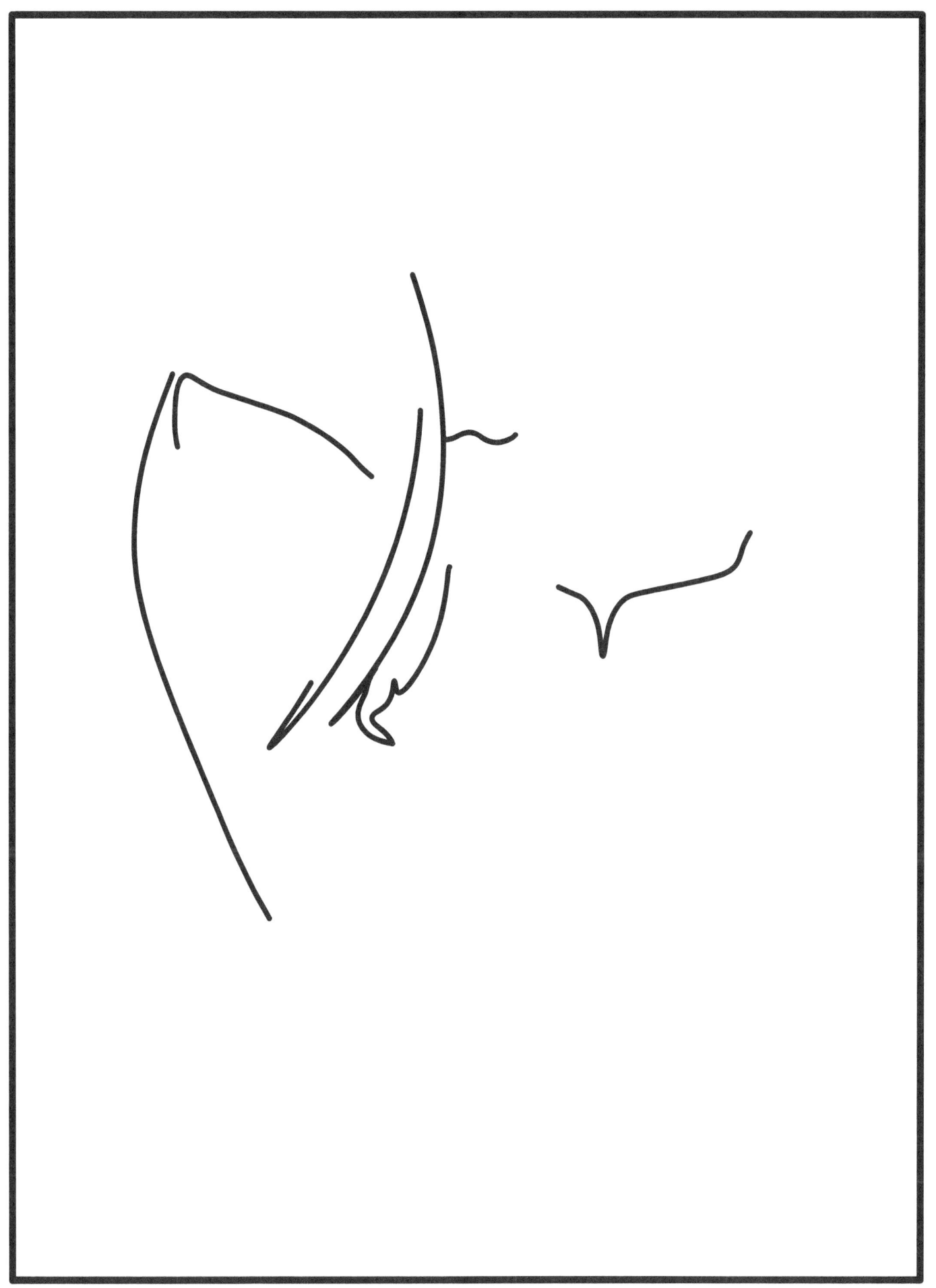

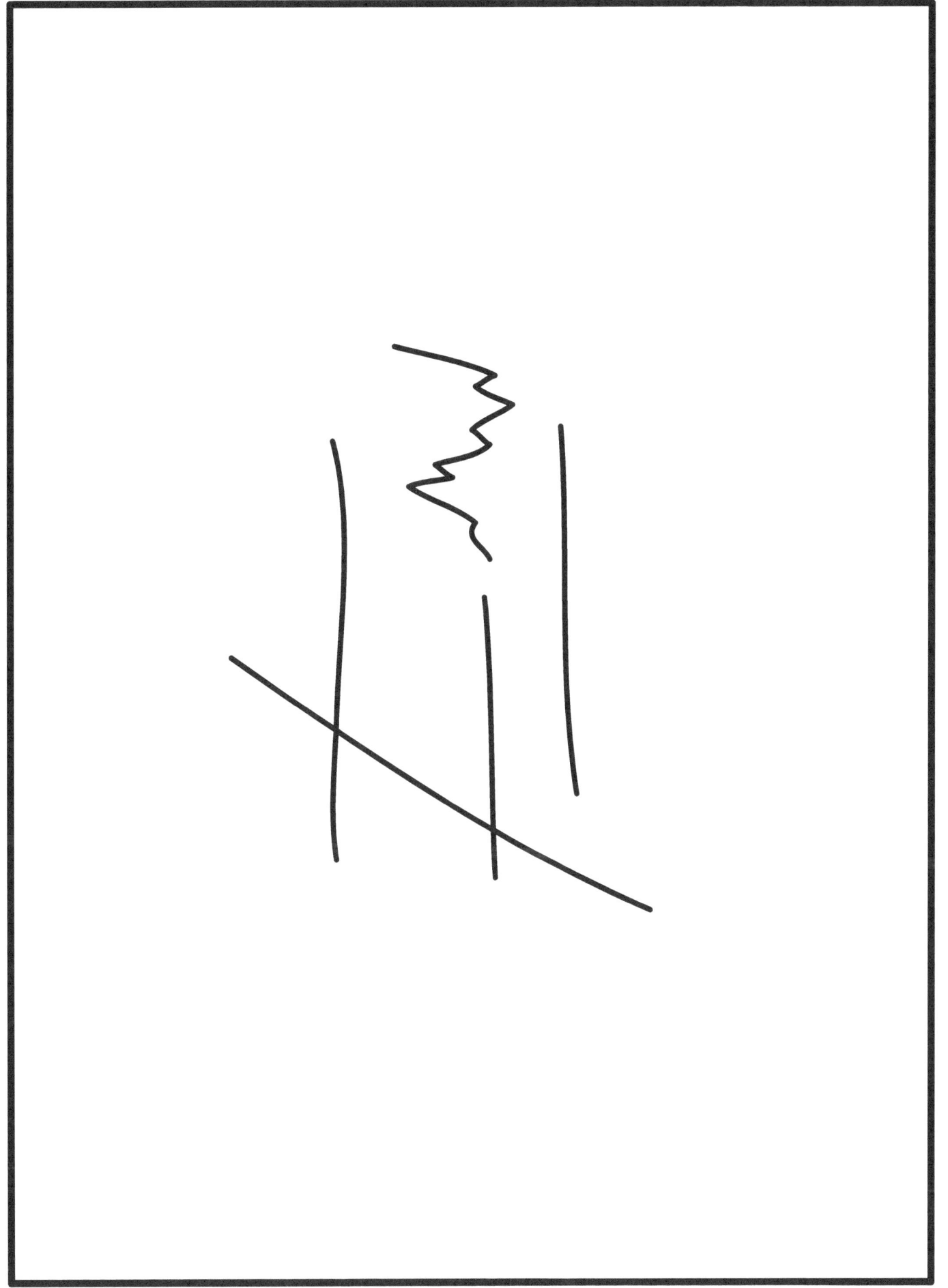

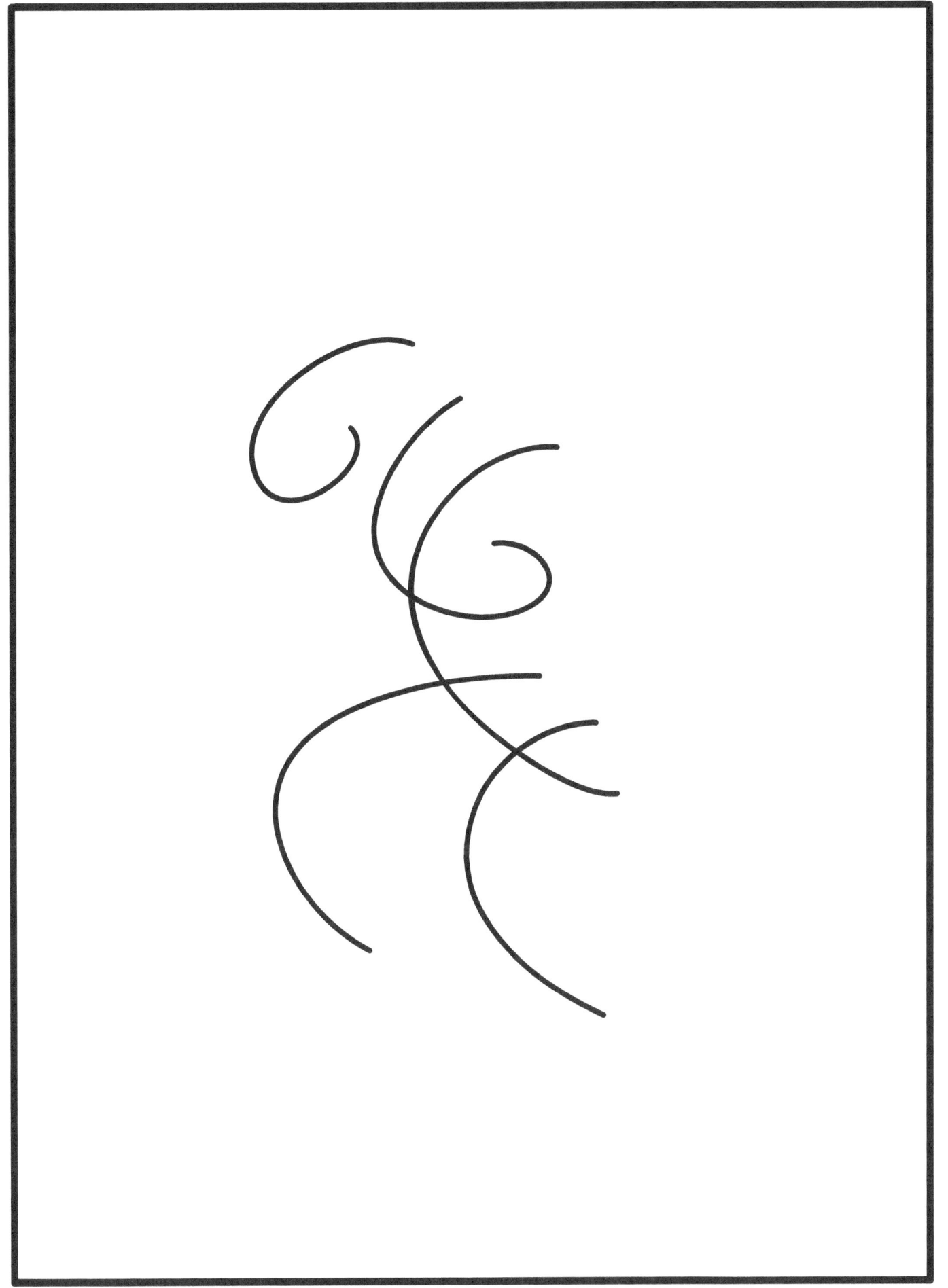

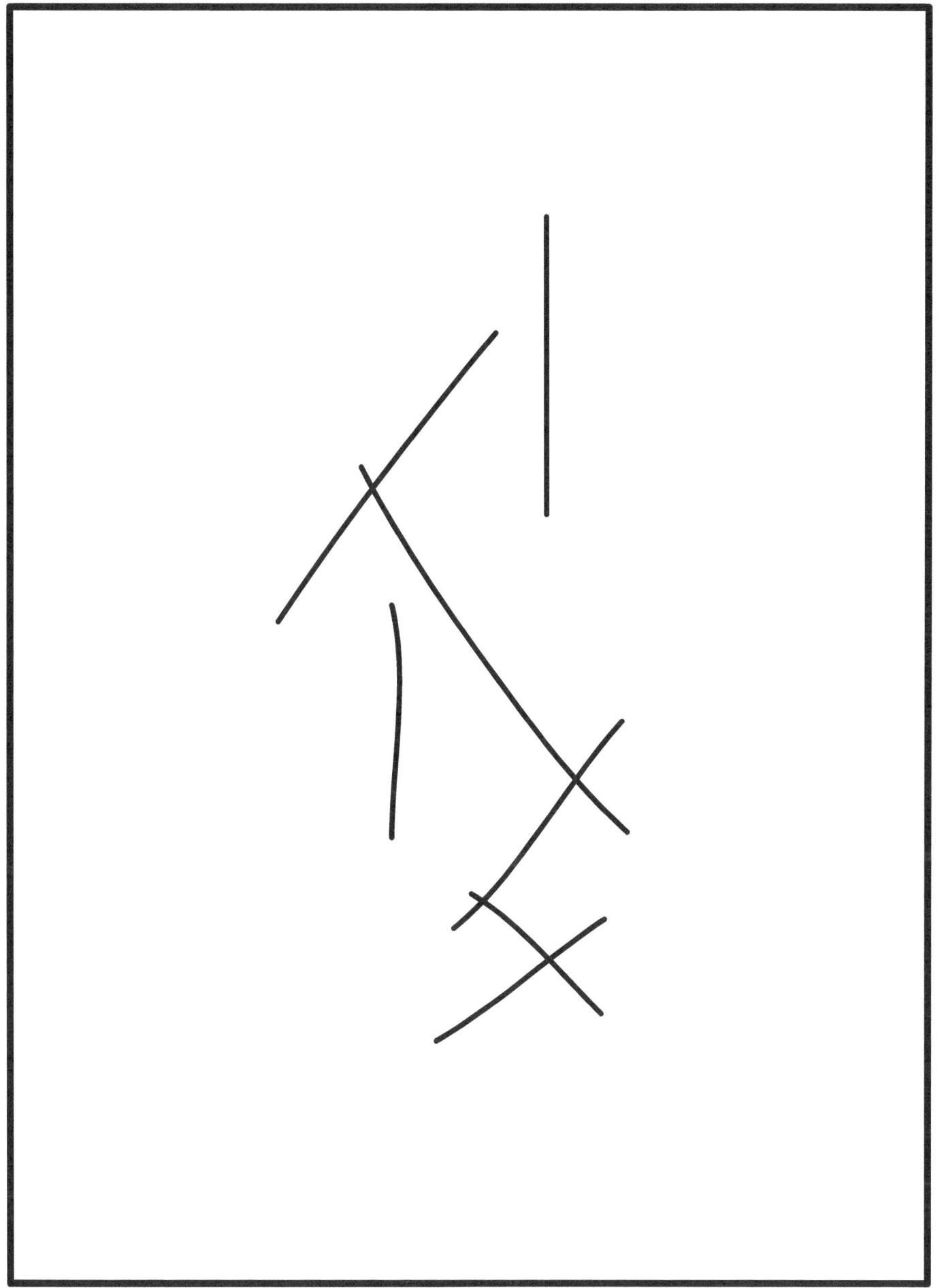

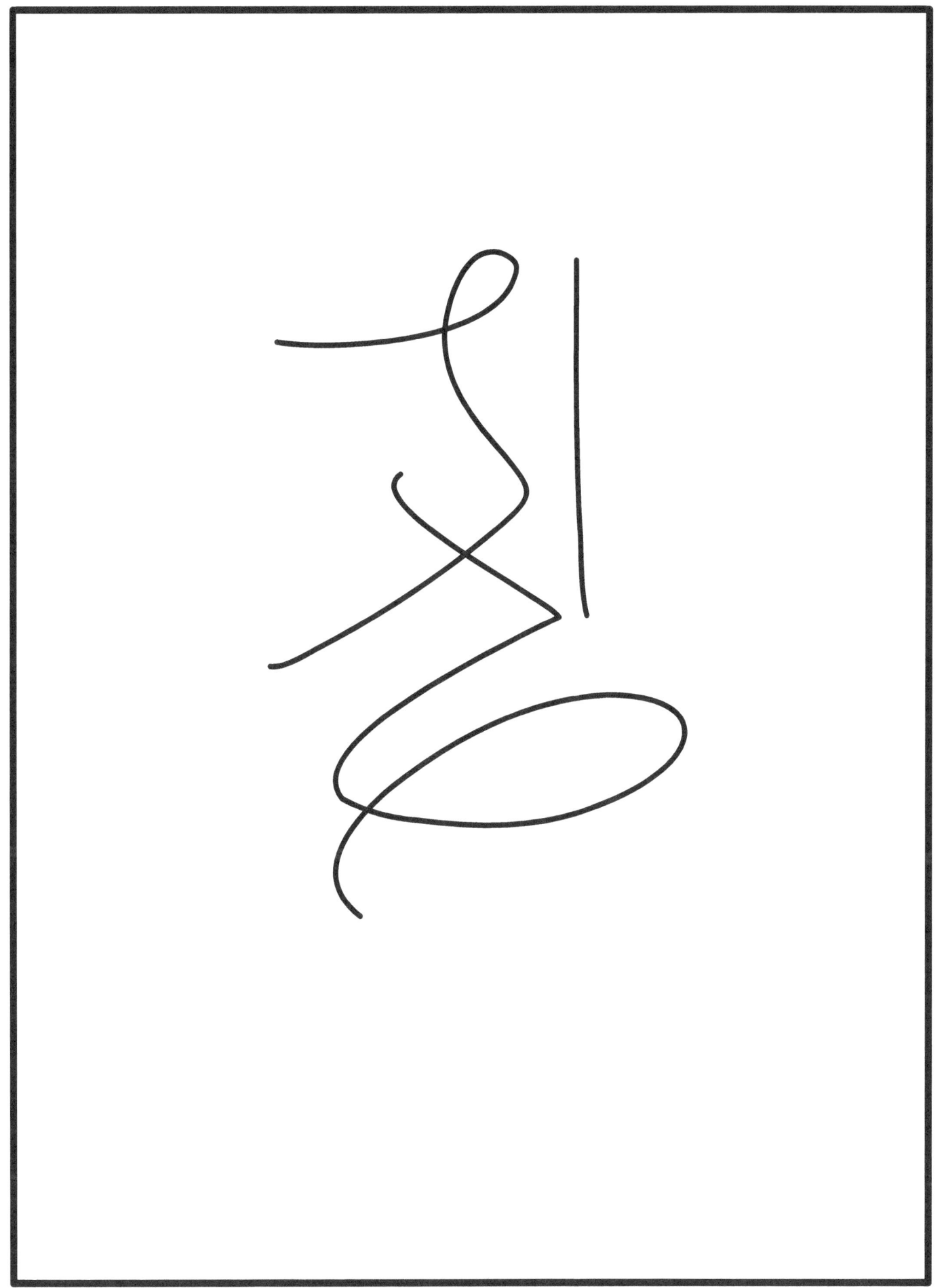

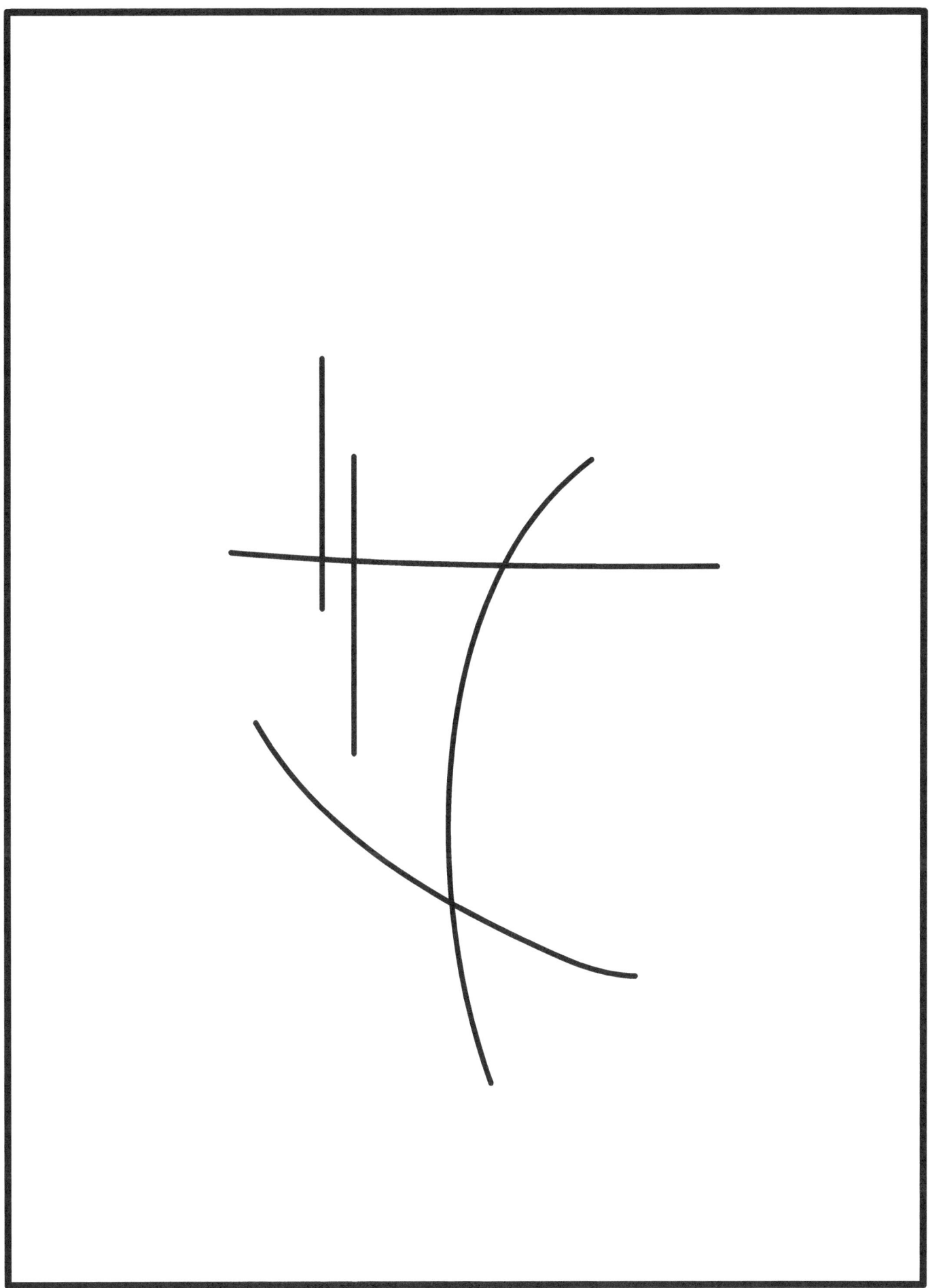

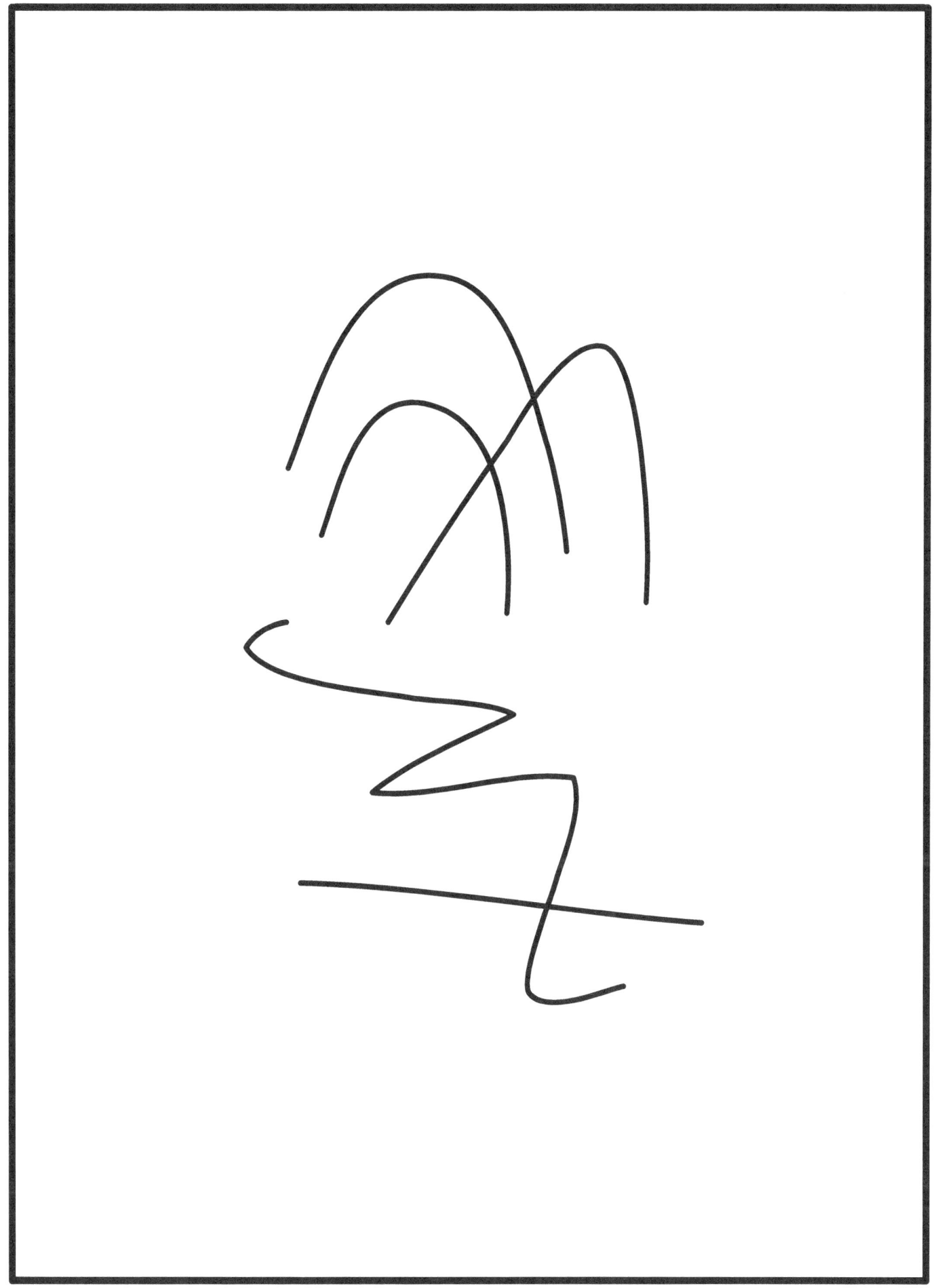

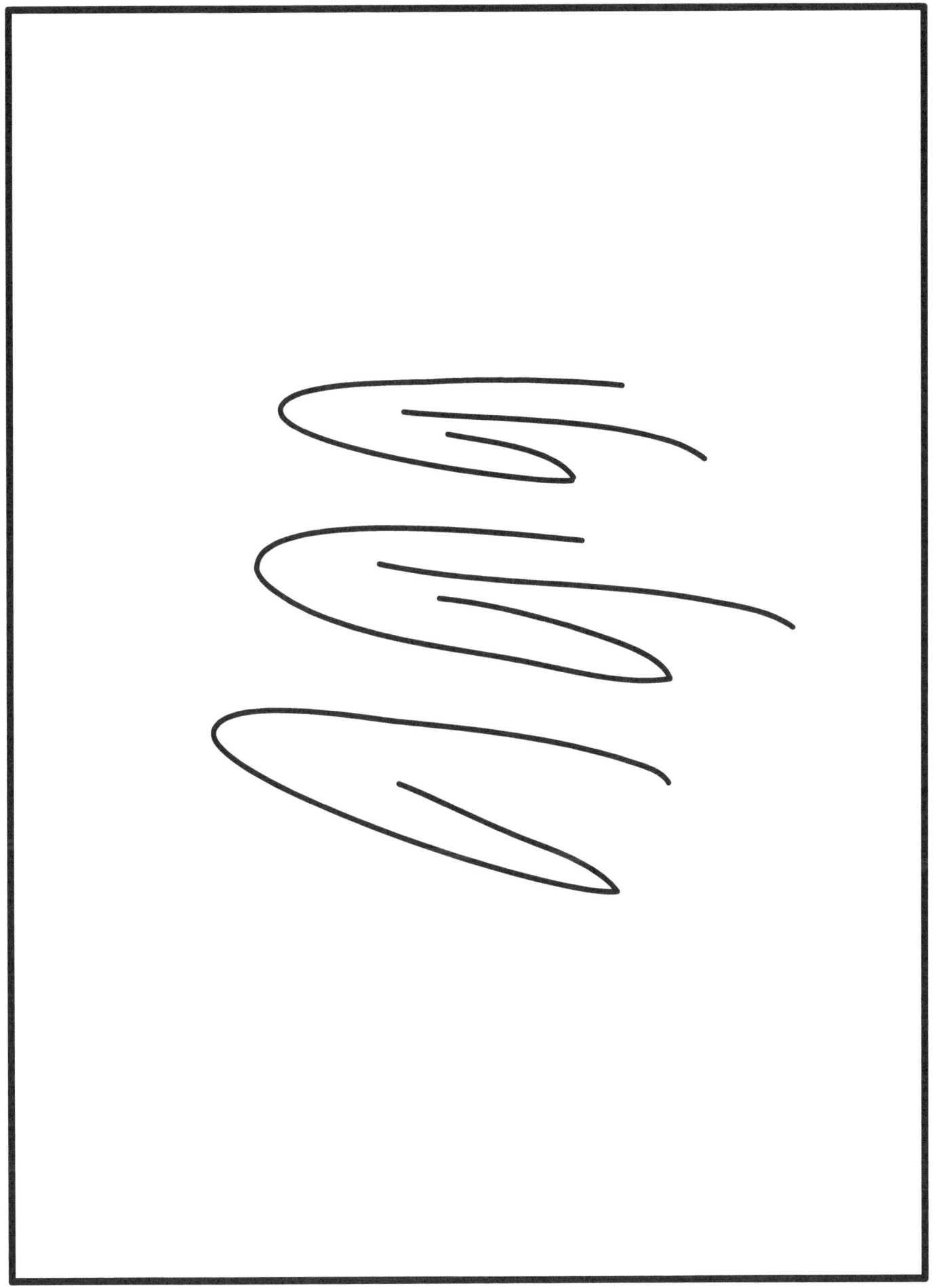

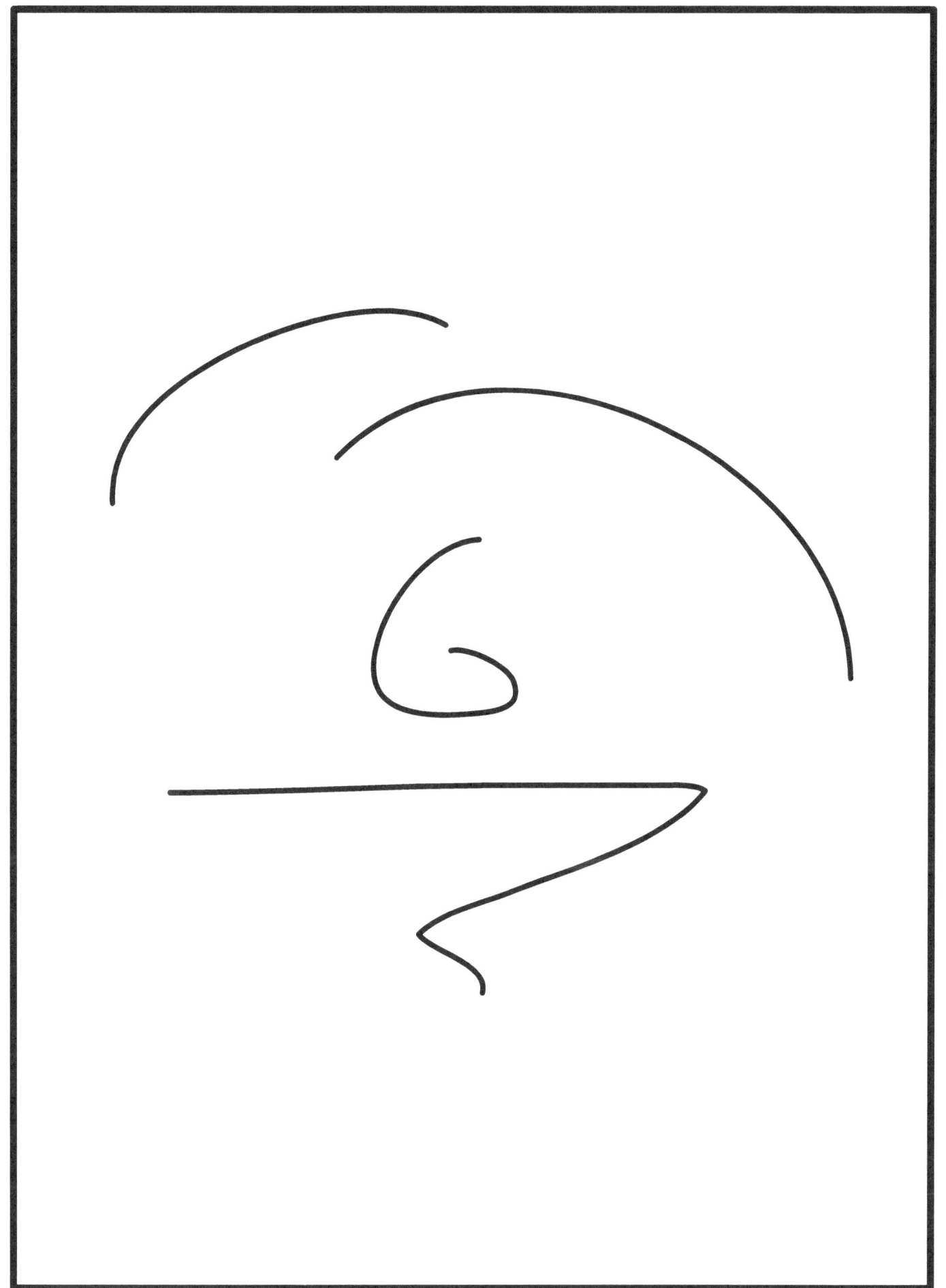

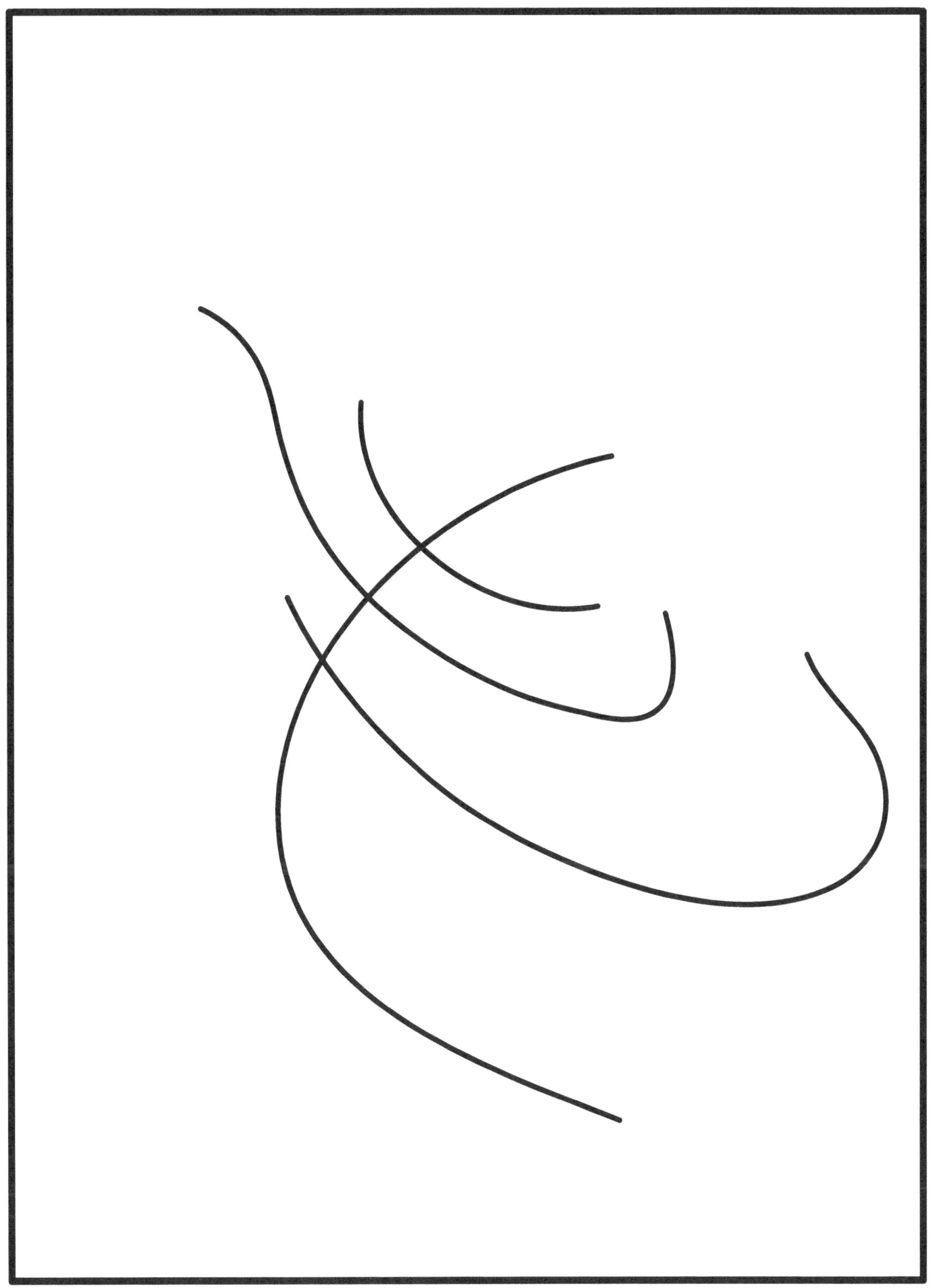

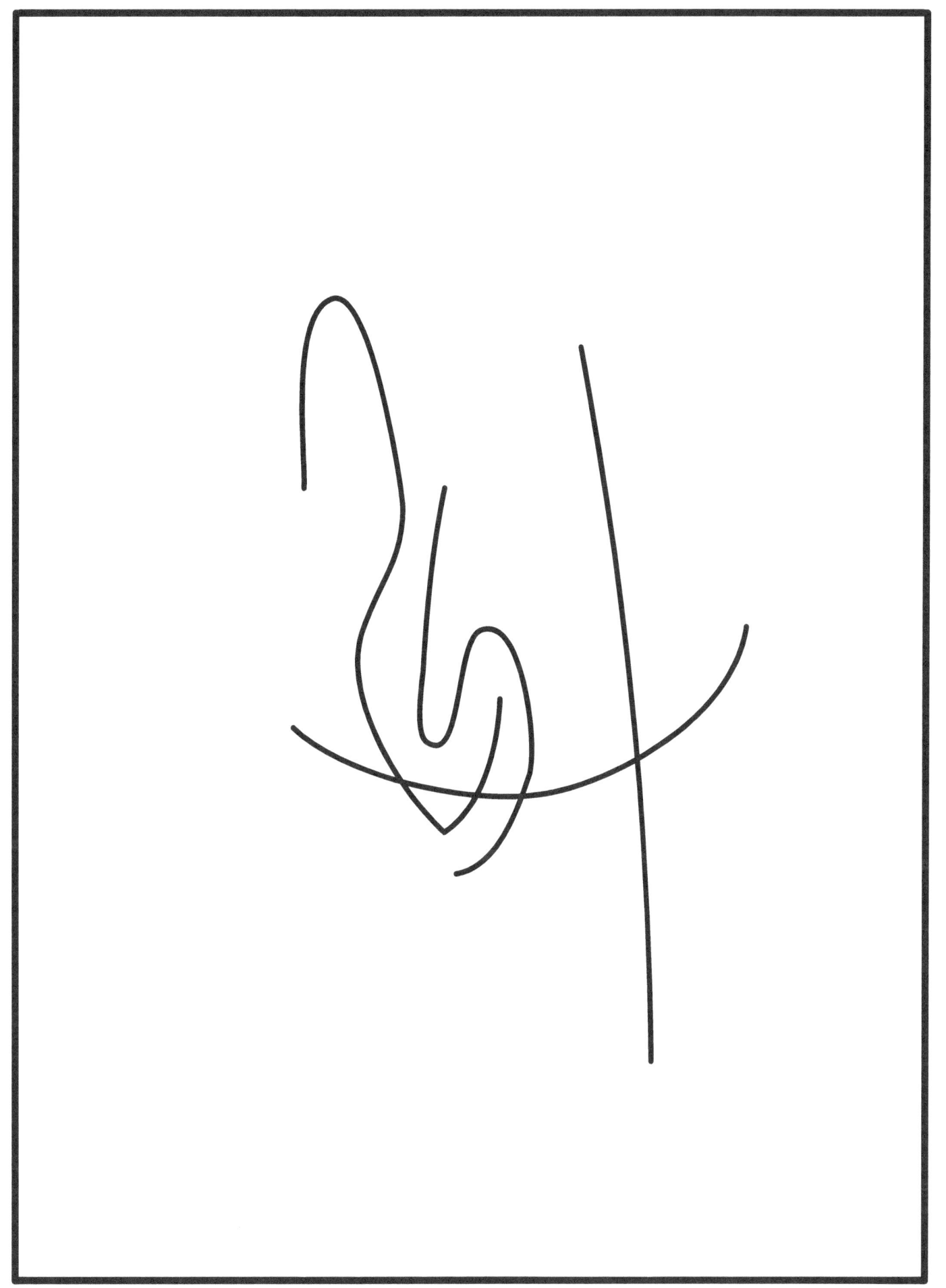

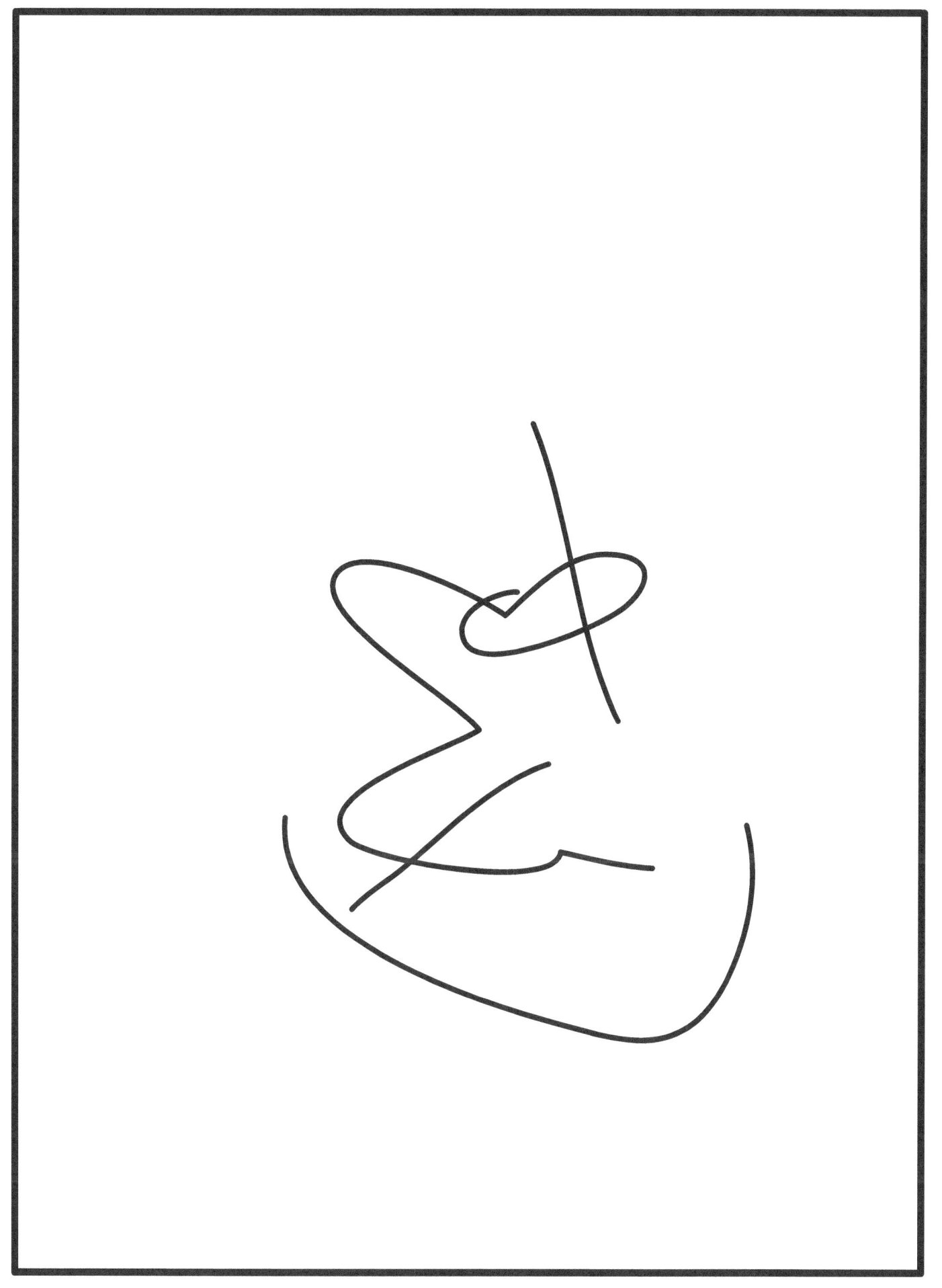

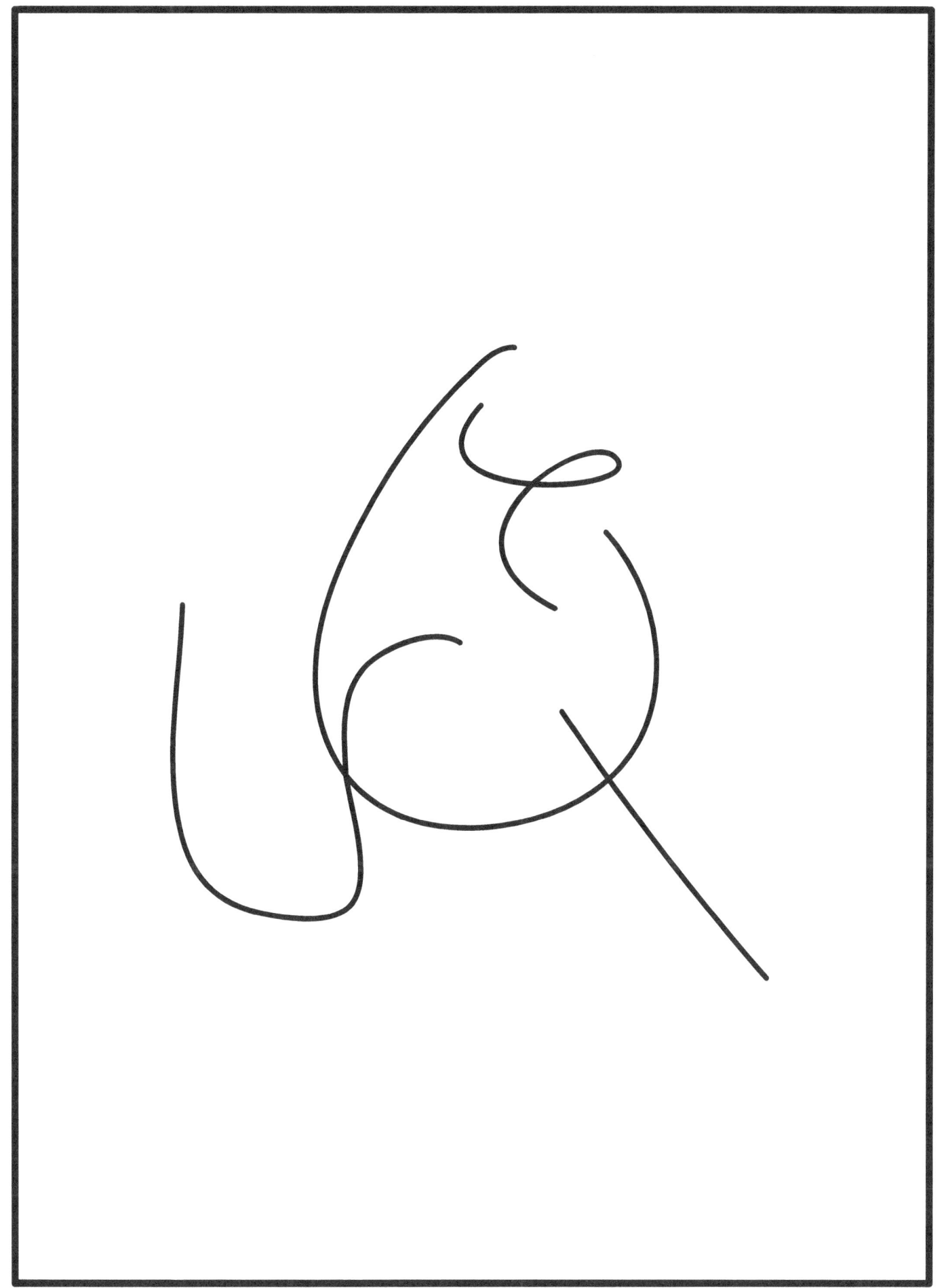

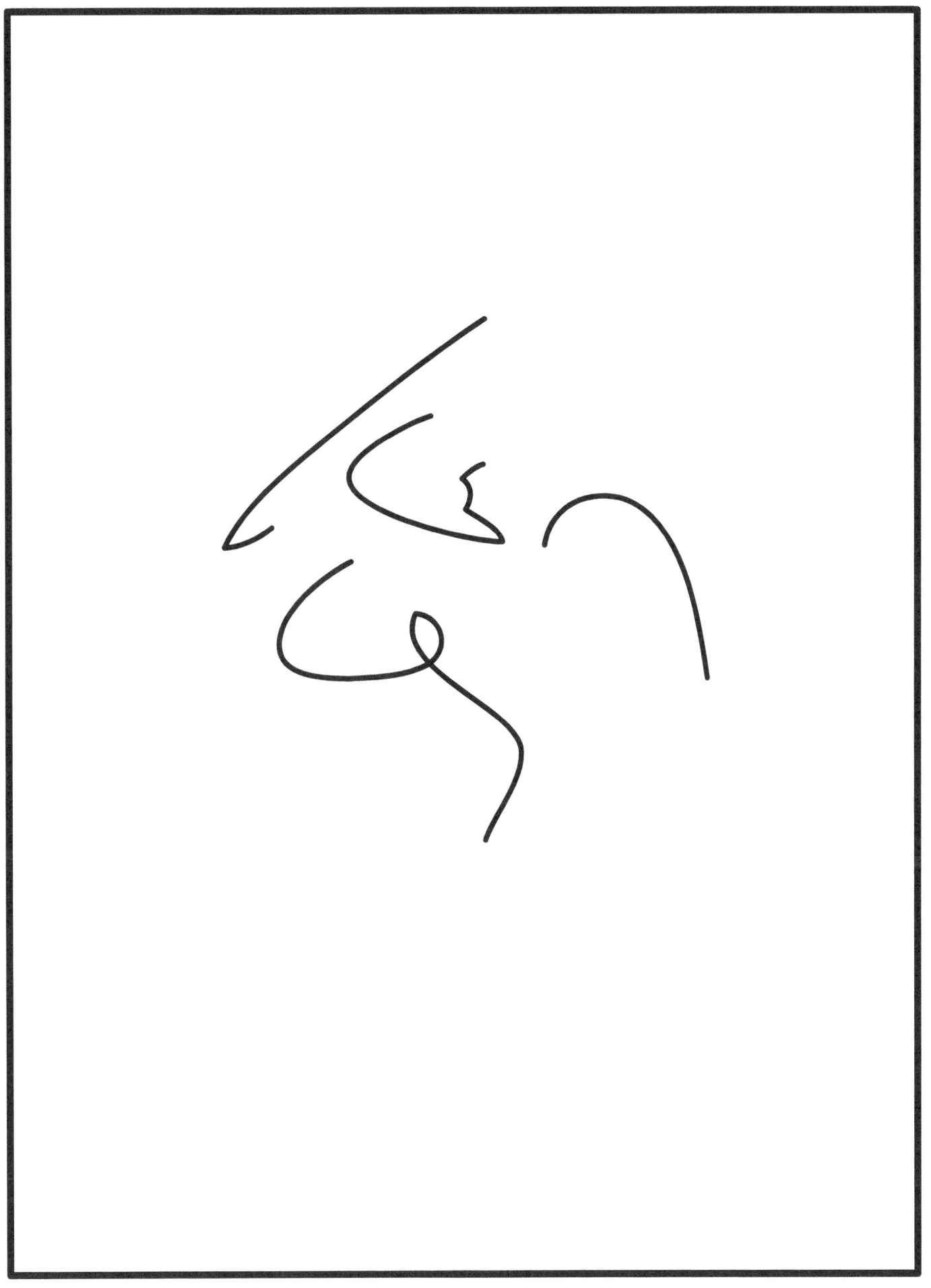

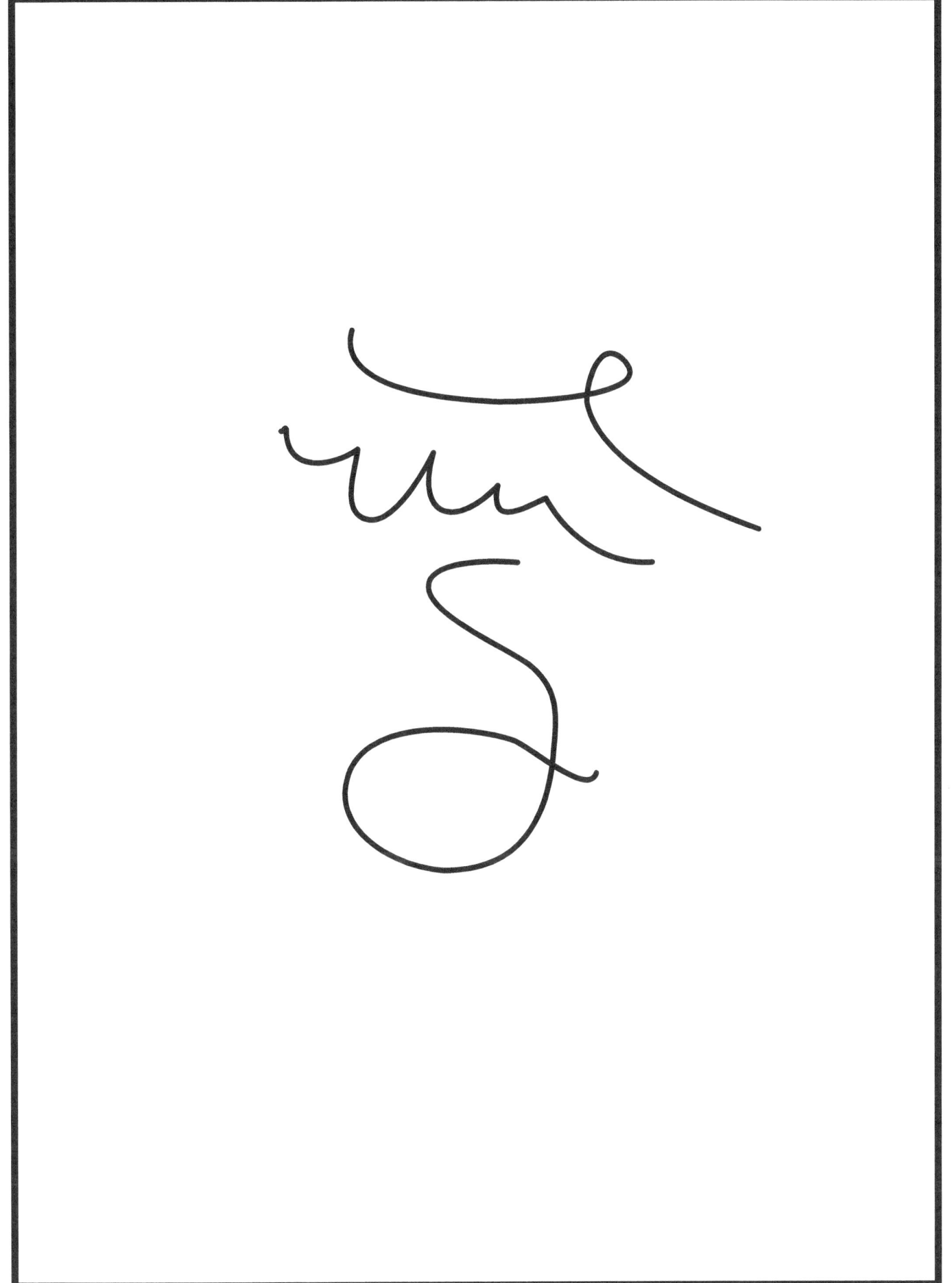

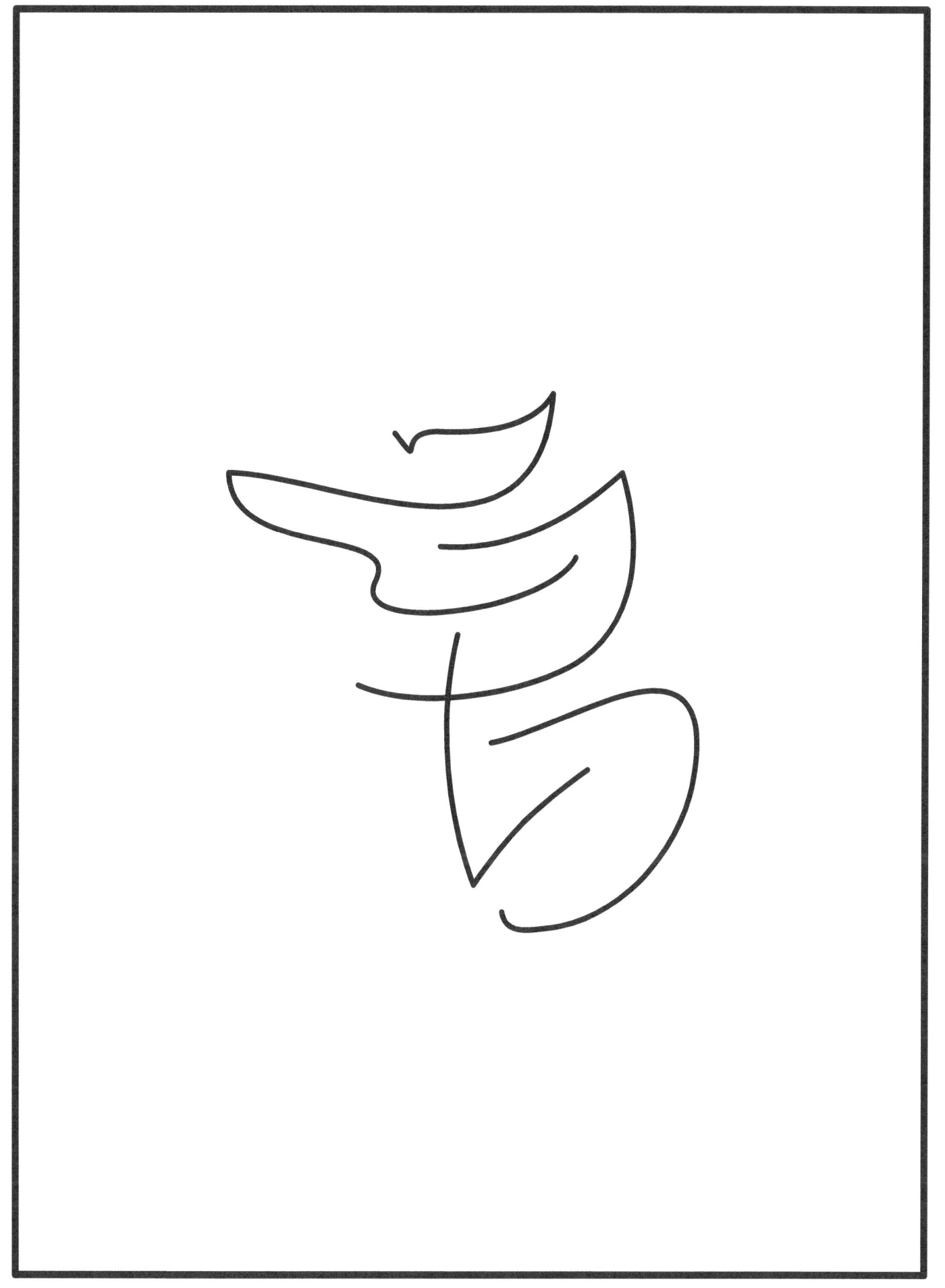